The Little Book of
HORSES & PONIES

Kate Brookes

www.alligatorbooks.co.uk

© 2006 Alligator Books Ltd

Published by Alligator Books Ltd
Gadd House, Arcadia Avenue
London N3 2JU

Printed in China
ISBN-13: 978-1-84239-966-8
ISBN-10: 1-84239-966-7

Contents

History on the hoof

The first recorded horses were very small and didn't really look much like modern-day horses. Eohippus, who evolved about 40 million years ago, was no bigger than a fox!

The first horsey-looking horses were Pliohippus and Equus. Equus, who evolved at around the same time as humans, is an ancient forebear of the modern horse. But Equus wouldn't make it as a horse today – he was only 12 hands. Horses must be at least 14.2 hands high; less than that is a pony.

Eohippus is sometimes called the 'dawn horse'.

From herds of Equus evolved the ancestors of the Arab, the Akhal-Teke and two British ponies – the Highland and the Exmoor. From these, over 200 breeds have developed through the years, including the tiny Falabella and the gentle giant Shire.

The stunning grey Arab is the most pure and ancient of all breeds.

Horses and us

Horses and humans have a very special relationship. Horses have served humans for thousands of years, helping us plough the fields, milling grain and moving people and goods across countries.

Horses took soldiers and guns to the front line of battles, then carried the wounded back. They have been heroes in harness and under saddle, and deserve lots of admiration and respect.

Mare and foal

But why do horses get on with us? Some experts think that it is because horses are herd animals. To keep the herd strong, horses must be sociable, affectionate, caring and cooperative. When horse and human get together, the horse remains true to his nature – friendly, loving and willing to work and help. When you next see horses or ponies in a field, really watch them. There is lots to learn about them and from them.

Humans almost hunted the ancient and wild Przewalski horse to extinction, now they protect it.

Horses were domesticated about 5,000 years ago, but never forget that every horse is a wild animal.

Points of note

Parts of a pony's or horse's body are called his points. Everyone in the horsey world uses these terms, so brush up on them so that you can tell the withers from the poll!

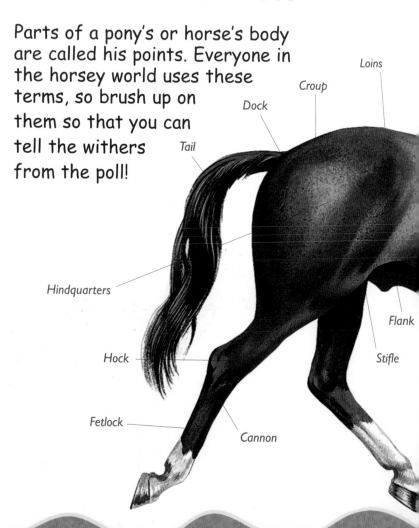

Loins

Croup

Dock

Tail

Hindquarters

Flank

Hock

Stifle

Fetlock

Cannon

Poll

Mane

Forelock

Cheek

Girth

Withers

Muzzle

Chin groove

Throat

Shoulder

Breast

Forearm

Knee

Elbow

Heel

How a horse looks, its balance and shape is called conformation. Experts look at the conformation to judge a pony's health and how it will perform.

9

Show your true colours

The colour of a pony or horse, along with a drawing of its markings, are needed for official identification when buying or selling a horse, and sometimes when entering competitions.

Bay: light to dark brown with black mane, tail and legs

Black: solid black all over; a true black has a black muzzle and skin

Brown: chocolate-brown coat, mane, tail and legs

Chestnut: light to dark reddish-brown

Dun: mouse-coloured coat often with black mane, tail and legs

Grey: mixture of white and black hairs

Palomino: lovely golden colour with lighter mane and tail

Piebald: black and white patches

Roan: mixture of black, brown or chestnut and white hair

Skewbald: white and patches of any colour except black

A pony can also be identified by a letter and number code freeze branded onto his skin, called a freezemark.

▲ Palomino is a colour, not a particular breed of horse.

◄ A pinto coat is a mix of piebald and skewbald, which is why a pinto is called a 'painted pony'.

Markings

White markings are found on the face and legs of many breeds, but pure breeds like Thoroughbreds and Arabs shouldn't have any marks at all. Foals are sometimes born with their markings, but others like the Appaloosa are born with a solid colour. Their markings appear later.

If a stripe marking stops at eye level and starts again on the forehead, it is a star-and-stripe marking.

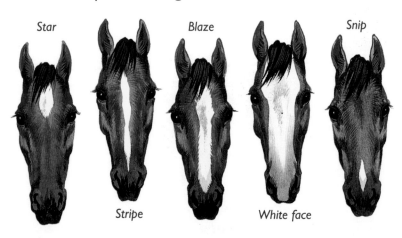

Star

Blaze

Snip

Stripe

White face

These are the five most common leg markings.

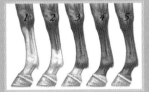

1. Stocking
2. Sock
3. Pastern
4. Heel
5. Coronet

Hoof colour varies from very pale to dark. Some ponies have three dark hooves and one white hoof!

To describe a horse as fleabitten is not rude. A fleabitten coat is one flecked with dark hair.

◄ No two Appaloosas are the same – their markings are totally unique. It is the horse version of a fingerprint!

13

Which pony?

There are about 206 breeds of horses, of which 67 are ponies. Here are some popular riding ponies.

Dales pony

Dales
Dales ponies are very strong, and were once used as pack horses to carry lead out of mines.

They stand at around 14 hands and their legs have feathers above the hooves (a crown of long hair).

Dartmoor
Dartmoor ponies have small ears, a long, full mane and grow to 12.2 hands. Sure-footed, they can live to an old age and are very calm ponies to ride.

Exmoor

Never judge a pony by his looks — it is his temperament that really counts.

If schooled properly when young, Exmoor ponies are excellent to ride. The Exmoor has prominent eyes and the coat has an unusual 'springy' texture.

Haflinger pony

Haflinger
You can't miss this pony with its chestnut coat and blonde-bombshell mane and tail! At 13.3 hands, the Haflinger is trustworthy and kind.

15

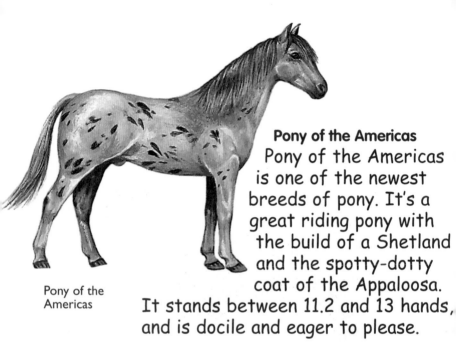

Pony of the
Americas

Pony of the Americas
Pony of the Americas is one of the newest breeds of pony. It's a great riding pony with the build of a Shetland and the spotty-dotty coat of the Appaloosa. It stands between 11.2 and 13 hands, and is docile and eager to please.

Shetland
Standing at ten hands, the Shetland is popular as a child's first mount. This breed is also used in carriage driving because of their strength and intelligence. A Shetland can be any colour.

Welsh Mountain

There are three types of Welsh Mountain pony and the Welsh Section B has been the first ride of many children. All Welsh ponies are intelligent, lively and strong. This breed is the most beautiful of all British ponies, which is why in countries like the USA the breed has become popular for showing, riding and harness driving. A Welsh pony stands between 12 and 13.2 hands.

Welsh mountain pony

Many of the ponies you may ride will be a mixture of different breeds (crossbred).

Gentle giants and miniatures

▶ In the late 1800s, a Shire
called 'Mammoth' became
the world's tallest horse.
He was a towering
21.2 hands!

Shire

For all their size and strength, Shires are gentle giants and easy to manage. Today, you are most likely to see Shires pulling agricultural machinery in working museums, or decked out in glistening horse brass hitched to an old-fashioned cart.

Falabella

These miniature horses (despite their size, Falabellas are horses) rarely grow taller than seven hands and make wonderful pets. The Falabella line started about 100 years ago when a small Thoroughbred was crossed with a tiny Shetland. The Falabella is not strong enough for riding.

▶ One of the smallest recorded Falabellas was 'Sugar-Dumpling'. This mare measured just five hands.

Horses for courses

Appaloosa

You can spot this American breed because of their spots! There are six Appaloosa patterns: snowflake, spotted, blanket, marble, leopard and frost. Reaching 15.2 hands, this breed can run quickly over long distances on uneven ground.

Arab

The easiest way to spot an Arab is to look at the face side-on – it dips below the eyes. Like the Thoroughbred, the Arab is fast, sure-footed, brave, intelligent and strong. Arabs are solid coloured and reach 14.2 to 15 hands.

Thoroughbred

The majestic Thoroughbred owes its strength, speed, intelligence and courage to careful breeding. But the world's fastest and most valuable breed is also very nervous. Thoroughbreds are always a solid colour and stand at 16 hands.

The Arab has been around for at least 5,000 years, and remains one of the purest breeds.

A beautiful Thoroughbred will take your breath away.

Dancing, prancing steeds

Some horses and ponies are born to high-step their way into your heart!

Andalusian

These Spanish horses are incredibly agile, which is why they are often found performing high-school dressage (Haute Ecole), and are also the mount for a bullfighter facing the bull!

Lipizzaner

Masters of dressage in the Spanish Riding School, it takes years to train moves like the tricky capriole. From a standing start, the horse leaps into the air, kicks out its hind legs, then lands exactly where it started.

The following four horses have unusual gaits (ways of walking) that set them apart.

* The **Tennessee Walking horse** has three very unique gaits, but one, the running walk, is a favourite with riders.

Icelandic pony

* When an **Icelandic pony** breaks into its 'pace' gait, the rider feels as if the pony is floating! The pony moves both legs on one side together so there is a moment when all feet float above the ground.

Hackney pony

*The **Missouri Fox** Trotter's claim to fame is his fox trot. Its hind legs trot while the front walk.

* The high-stepping gait of a **Hackney pony** is formed by bringing the hocks (ankle joints) high up under the body.

Talk the horse talk

Here is some more horsey talk for you to learn. Knowing what the initials mean will help you to understand all those 'Pony for Sale' ads!

Colt	Young male
Filly	Young female
Foal	Pony or horse less than one year old
Gelding	Male who has had his testicles removed
Mare	Female horse or pony
Stallion	Male who has not been gelded
Yearling	Horse or pony who is one year old

C/S	Cob size
DR	Dressage
F/S	Full size
LDR	Long distance riding
LR	Leading rein
ODE	One day event
PB	Part bred
PC	Pony Club
P/S	Pony size
RC	Riding Club
RP	Ridden pony
SJ	Show jumper
SP	Show pony
TB	Thoroughbred
X	Cross bred
XC	Cross Country

What does your pony need?

Even if you could be with your pony 24/7, you may still feel there's not enough hours in the day. There are always chores to do and fun to be had.

But while you hanker to plait your pony's tail and practise jumps, here's what tops your pony's wish-list:

Ponies have a built-in clock and enjoy routine. Do each task in the same order and at the same time every day.

- Good feed of the right sort and quantity at the right times.

- Fresh water all the time.

- Pasture and stabling that is safe and secure.

- The company of other ponies and horses. Everyone needs mates, don't they?

- Exercise for fitness and fun with someone he respects and loves (you!).

- A daily groom and check, and regular shoeing.

No wonder pony people are so busy... and so happy! Read on to find out about these pony must-haves.

Be feed wise

A pony who lives out all the time can spend 16 hours a day slowly grazing to fill his small stomach. But if your pony is sometimes stabled, sometimes in the field, the top feeding tip is: little and often. This may mean two to four feeds a day depending on the richness of the grazing grass and the amount of exercise he gets.

Camargue horses survive in the wild feeding on the rough grass of salt marshes.

Ponies can choke on small chunks of fruit and vegetables. Cut apples into quarters and carrots lengthways, never into rounds.

Your pony's diet should include:

Menu

* Roughage – grass, hay, haylage (hay and silage mix) and chaff (chopped straw/hay).

* Hard feeds – oats, maize, bran and barley.

* Fruit and vegetables – apples, carrots, turnips and parsnips.

* Fresh water – a pony can drink up to 20 litres (about equal to two large buckets) of water a day; a horse around 40 litres.

* Supplements – small amounts of these ingredients are added to hard feed. Garlic powder is a supplement that repels flies. Smelly!

Grass roots

Ponies love being turned out into a field and will show their pleasure by galloping off, neighing in delight and having a good roll, usually in the muddiest puddle!

Here's how to get the field-good factor:
Walk the field at least once a week, digging up poisonous plants, checking fences, picking up muck and removing any rubbish blown or dumped into the field. At the same time, make sure the water supply is not blocked and give the water bucket a clean.

Ragwort is poisonous for ponies and horses.

Make sure there are no yew or oak trees edging the field. Yew leaves and unripe acorns are poisonous.

...n you spot the things above that make this a ...od home-field for a pony? Here's what to look ...r: good fencing; a gate with a catch; trees, ...dging and a barn for shelter and protection; ...ort grass for grazing; plenty of water and feed ...oughs; and, for company, a couple of sheep.

To keep a pony at grass year-round, you'll need a field of over half a hectare (about 1.5 acres).

Best of stable mates

A stable is not just 'home' for a pony, it is where you will groom, prepare feed, store tack, muck out and just hang out with your favourite four-legged friend. A stable has to be large enough for the pony to walk around and to lie down. It should also be airy. An awning will give shade and protect the pony from driving rain.

A stabled pony who is bored or unhappy may box walk (walk round and round), crib bite and suck in air, or weave (rock from side to side). For warmth and comfort, the stable floor is covered with a deep layer of straw, wood shavings or shredded paper bedding.

Don't disturb cobwebs in the stable - they are natural fly catchers!

Mucking out – removing dung and wet bedding from the stable – needs to be done twice a day. Push a fork under the droppings, shake to remove clean bedding, then tip the muck into a basket or barrow. Wet bedding can be scooped up with a fork or shovel. Smooth out the bedding or top up with new bedding.

Shavings fork for mucking out shavings

Shovel

Basic stable kit:

Four-pronged fork for mucking out straw

Wheelbarrow

Stiff broom

Plastic or wire basket

Grooming

Ponies aren't fussed about being squeaky clean, but who doesn't want their pony to look drop-dead gorgeous? Grooming isn't just about looking good, it also stimulates a pony's blood flow and you can check your pony for cuts and bites.

A once-daily grooming must-do is picking out your pony's feet with a hoof pick. Another is brushing the body and face to remove dried mud that will rub against tack and cause chaffing.

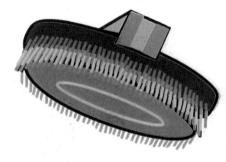

When brushing, use quick firm strokes — ponies can be ticklish!

• Stiff dandy brush removes dried mud, especially on winter coats. Never use on a pony's face.

• Soft body brush and rubber curry comb for body and face.

• Sponges for eyes, nose and lips, and dock.

• Tail and mane can be groomed with a water brush and mane and tail combs.

• Sweat scraper will remove sweat and water after exercise and a bath.

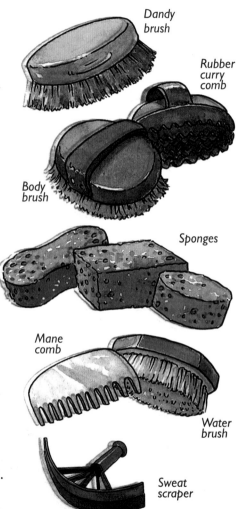

Dandy brush

Rubber curry comb

Body brush

Sponges

Mane comb

Water brush

Sweat scraper

Tip-top pony

A happy, healthy pony has:

• warm, pricked ears

. clear and shiny eyes, and the surrounding membrane is a salmon-pink colour

• clean, pink nostrils

• a glossy coat that lies flat

A pony needs hooves trimmed and new shoes every four to six weeks. The farrier may rasp a pony's teeth at the same time.

You can tell a lot about a pony by reading his body language.

Ears drooped and cold – pain

Mouth stiff, lips tight – pain

Ears back and flat to head – frightened or angry

Low hung tail – sleepy, fearful or in pain

Tail swishing wildly – confused or anxious

Nudging with nosetip, mouth closed – lots of discomfort

Pawing the ground – 'I'm bored'

Resting a front leg – never a good sign, so call the vet

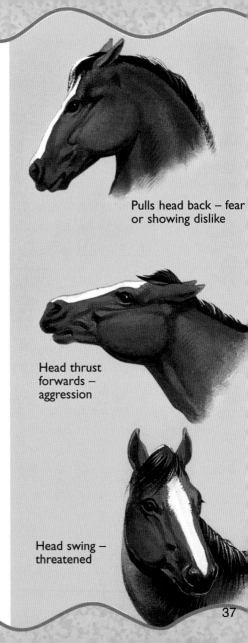

Pulls head back – fear or showing dislike

Head thrust forwards – aggression

Head swing – threatened

37

The tack room

A saddle and bridle are the essential bits of tack
that help you control the pony when riding. A general
purpose saddle is for all-round riding and is held on
the pony's back by the girth. Your feet rest in stirrup
irons that are attached to stirrup leathers. The way
you sit in the saddle tells the pony when you want him
to walk, trot, canter, gallop or jump.

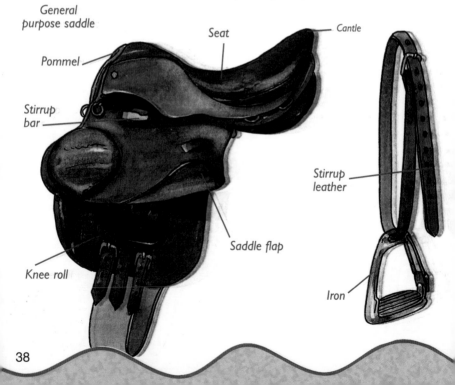

General
purpose saddle

Seat

Cantle

Pommel

Stirrup
bar

Stirrup
leather

Saddle flap

Knee roll

Iron

The bridle is a web of leather straps and buckles that fits onto the pony's head. The reins are part of the bridle and they connect you to the pony. When you squeeze on the reins, the bit makes more contact with a corner of the pony's mouth, and the pony will turn or stop.

The most important thing about tack is that it fits correctly. Get the advice of an experienced rider before buying tack and when tacking up.

Snaffle bridle

Throatlash

Headpiece

Browband

Cheekpiece

Noseband

Bit

Snaffle bit

Reins

Tacking up

Ponies love routine, so tack up in the same order each time and your pony will know what is coming next.

1. Check tack and have it handy.

2. Tie up pony with headcollar and lead rope and pick out feet and brush to remove dried mud.

Buckleguard

3. Stand at pony's left side and slide on saddle rug, then lower saddle gently onto back.

4. Attach girth to right side of saddle, then go around pony and bring girth under the belly and buckle to saddle.

Fasten the girth and pull down buckle guards. Check girth again after mounting.

. Stand close on the pony's
eft and place reins over his
ead. Hold the top of the
ridle in your right hand.
Undo headcollar and buckle
oosely around pony's neck.

. Hold bridle in front of
ony and place bit in pony's
outh with left hand.

. Gently pull headpiece
ver pony's ears and bring
orelock over the browband.

. Fasten throatlash, then
oseband.

. Bring down stirrup irons,
emove headcollar and hold
he pony's head while an
xperienced rider checks
he tack.

A pony should not
be exercised for
60-90 minutes after eating.

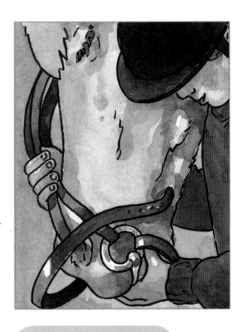

Encourage the pony to take
the bit by slipping thumb
into upper corner of mouth.
There are no teeth here, but
it does take practice!

First lessons – walk on

You've got to feel confident whatever you're doing with your pony. A pony will sense fear and may play

Your first lessons are about being confident mounti sitting in the saddle, holding the reins and giving yo pony clear signals.

How a rider sits in the saddle is called the 'seat'.

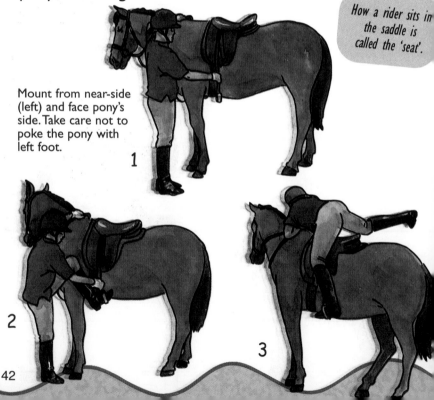

Mount from near-side (left) and face pony's side. Take care not to poke the pony with left foot.

1

2

3

Before you can ride off, your teacher will make you do exercises in the saddle to help your posture and confidence.

You should be sitting so that a straight line can be drawn through ear, shoulder, hip and heel. Toes should point forwards.

Horses have four gaits – walk, trot, canter and gallop – and it's your job to communicate what you want the pony to do. This is done using your hands, legs, seat and voice.

To signal a pony to walk, press legs evenly against the pony's side, sit tall and say 'walk on'. A pony will stop when you squeeze on the reins, pull gently and say 'halt'. Squeezing gently on the right or left rein will tell the pony you want to turn right or left.

Hot to trot

When a pony walks you can count 1-2-3-4 in time with his leg movements. In a trot, the count is 1-2 because the pony moves pairs of diagonally opposite feet. To tell the pony to go from walk to trot – shorten the reins and squeeze legs firmly against the pony's sides and say 'Trot on'.

Go from trot to canter on a curve.

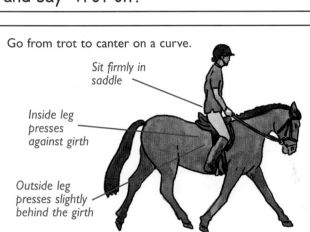

Sit firmly in saddle

Inside leg presses against girth

Outside leg presses slightly behind the girth

Cantering
The canter is a 1-2-3 gait and is a smoother ride than a trot. When cantering, there is a moment when all of the pony's feet are off the ground.

In the rising trot, you move up and down in rhythm with the pony.

A pony needs to be totally fit to gallop.

Galloping

The gallop is a 1-2-3-4 gait where you lean forwards out of the saddle, squeeze legs against the pony's sides and shorten the reins. The most important thing about the gallop is being able to confidently stop the pony!

Safety first

• Only ride when you and the pony are fit and his shoes are in good condition.

• Never ride-out on damaged tack. Get someone to check you have tacked up correctly.

• Tell someone where you are going and when you will return.

• Always wear a hard hat.

• In poor light, wear reflective gear – arm bands, gloves and jacket for you; exercise blanket and leg bands for him.

• Never ride when icy, don't trot downhill and don't canter on tarmac.

• Follow the rules of the road and obey all traffic signs. Give clear hand signals after checking for traffic in all directions and always be considerate to other road users.

• Follow the country code when off-road.

It's show time!

Competing is a big commitment whether you're entering a novice (beginners') class at a local riding club event or showjumping at the highest level. Getting you and a pony to a show looking great, feeling fit and ready to perform takes lots of planning.

If you're ready for a show, you and the pony work as a team, are confident and calm, know your paces and routines, trust each other, and have worked hard at schooling and training.

Before competing, you should visit lots of shows as a spectator to see what happens. You should also take the pony to get him used to the noise and activity.

Show classes

There are many classes, levels and types of competitions for novice riders. Some are about breed, others about riding performance or turn out, but many are just for fun!

Here's a guide to show turns:

Some shows require registration papers, membership, or for you to qualify first. Events run by riding centres or local clubs usually want just an entry fee.

Showing – judges check for looks (how closely the pony matches his breed type, called conformation), behaviour and movement. You can show your pony in-hand (you walk, trot and stand alongside) or ridden. Leading rein showing is for young riders who need someone to lead the pony. In ridden showing, you will ride in, dismount, unsaddle and show in-hand.

Judges assess looks, but even the best judges can't resist a pony with star quality!

Tack and turn out – this is all about being tacked and dressed properly. Leather should gleam, buckles and bit sparkle, and you and your pony should be groomed to perfection. There are strict rules about tack and turn out, so make sure you check first.

Riding classes – judges are looking at your position and your control of the pony, as well as how the pony moves and behaves. For this class, you and your pony perform a short routine including walk, trot, canter on both legs and a stand square (you halt the pony who doesn't move off until instructed). The secret to a high score is to be relaxed and to keep the routine simple.

Jumping – if you're a novice, enter the clear-round jumps where all successful entries receive a rosette. For fun, try Chase Me Charlie where riders follow each other over a jump that is gradually raised.

Don't get hung up on rosettes – your pony certainly doesn't care!

At all times be sensitive to your pony's needs. Too much competing and the strain of travelling can ruin a good pony.

Gymkhanas – these are about having fun while encouraging the agility and confidence of pony and rider. There are mounted games and races like the sack race (you get in the sack, not the pony!), apple bobbing, and lead and ride. If you enter a gymkhana, be prepared for lots of speedy mounting and dismounting.

World Class

You may be doing novice classes now, but your dreams may lie in one of these equestrian sports, perhaps even at Olympic level!

Dressage
Known as 'ballet on horseback', dressage is a riding test consisting of graceful moves in a set pattern. The rider is judged on her seat and position; the horse on his movement and obedience. Some of the hardest moves are trotting on the spot (piaffe), turning on the spot (pirouette) and trotting in slow motion (passage). Even young riders, though, perform dressage moves like circles and loops.

Showjumping

Watching the best showjumpers is breathtaking as they clear uprights, parallels, gates and walls. Rider and horse are faulted (lose points) if a bar is knocked down, the horse refuses a jump or if horse or rider fall.

Eventing

This is one of the most dangerous sports in the world and it is a test of bravery, endurance, speed, accuracy and obedience. In eventing, horse and rider do dressage, cross-country and showjumping. The cross-country section includes fields, roads and tracks, jumps, ditches, walls and water obstacles!

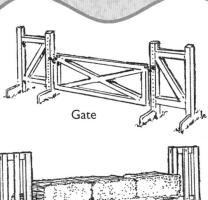
Gate

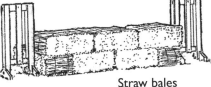
Straw bales

Planks

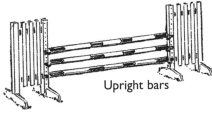
Upright bars

Endurance riding is becoming popular. One Australian rider, rode bare-back for over 11 hours. Ouch!

Teaming up

Some team games on horseback go back thousands of years and were originally a way of testing horsemanship. The mounted team games played at gymkhanas develop the skills that you need to play these highly competitive sports.

Polo is the fastest game in the world and done at a cracking gallop throughout. The aim of the game is to knock a ball into the opposing team's goal by whacking it with a long stick called a mallet.

Though always called polo ponies, they aren't actually ponies at all — they're horses!

Each team has four players. The reigning polo champions are the Argentine team mounted on Crillo X Thoroughbred horses.

Polo mallet

Polocrosse is a mixture of polo and lacrosse. Instead of hitting the ball with a stick, a net at the end of the stick is used to scoop up, catch and toss the ball into the opposing team's goal. Not as easy as it sounds when only one player on each team can score goals.

Polocrosse net

Horseball

One of the newest mounted games is called horseball. It has been described as playing netball and rugby while riding a horse! The aim is to grab hold of the ball by its handles and toss it into a netball-type hoop.

...and they're off!

The joy of seeing a horse run like the wind has thrilled riders and spectators for thousands of years. But flat racing (a race over a flat course) became the huge sport that it is today when the Thoroughbred was introduced to Britain and the Quarter Horse was developed in the USA. Horse racing is not just about colourful jockeys on sleek, powerful steeds, there are also speed tests for Arabs and, in North America, for tiny Shetland ponies!

The peaked cap worn by jockeys is a copy of the bronze ones worn by ancient Roman chariot drivers. The bronze cap, though, wasn't covered in colourful silks!

Steeplechasing is a winter sport. The first steeplechase was in Ireland when two men on Hunters (a type of horse) raced between two church steeples! Modern steeplechase races occur on 7.2 kilometre-long courses set with very difficult fences. Sadly, many horses and riders are injured in steeplechases.

One of the most famous steeplechase races is the Pardbicka in the Czech Republic. There are 30 awesome fences between start and finish!

In training

Here are some tips that will help you and your pony become a top team at shows.

- Start early to spread training over a long period. Two training sessions a week are enough.

- Be patient! Ponies don't like being hurried.

- Get advice on how to adjust your pony's feed while he's training and competing.

- Think ahead! You have to know what to do before it happens. Showjumpers, for example, look at the next jump even before the last is cleared.

- Never give up on a pony! If a pony refuses to do something, encourage him to try again. Do the same task in a different way or in smaller bits.

- Praise him when he gets something right. Don't punish him because he gets something wrong.

Never reward or punish bad behaviour, but always reward good behaviour. This rider will give her pony a treat the moment he steps up the ramp and into the lorry.

A pony will perform differently when away from his usual schooling arena. Get him used to new places.

Pony makeover

It may seem unfair, but when preparing for a show it's the pony that gets all the attention!

Grooming should start a week before the show. You may need to book a farrier for shoeing, the vet to rasp the pony's teeth or someone to clip the coat. The mane may need to be thinned (pulled) and the tail trimmed to below the hocks (banged).

Pulling a mane

Then, there's washing and brushing and hoof cleaning. It's a good idea to wash the tail and mane a few days before a show to avoid a bad hair day! All this, as well as checking and cleaning the tack and getting the pony's travelling gear together. It's a very busy time!

Brushing in a quartermark
using a stencil

The night before the
show, leave the pony
in a clean stable.
If there's muck,
a sparkling pony will
roll in it.

Start early on the show
morning to plait the mane,
forelock or tail. Then, after
grooming, brush in a pattern
(a quartermark) on his
quarters.

At the show, brush oil onto
the hooves, dust chalk onto
white leg marks and dab a
little Vaseline onto the nose
and around the eyes.

In strict showing
classes, British native
ponies shouldn't have
their hair plaited or
trimmed. Always check
with the breed society for
the rules.

It's a magical world

You know there is something magical about horses, but do you realise just how magical they are?

• The unicorn was a horse-like creature with a long horn in the middle of his forehead. Legend says the unicorn would use his horn to test if a liquid was poisonous.

• In Greek mythology, Xanthos was the first talking horse.

• A horseshoe is thought to protect and bring good luck. But it must be pointed upwards in a 'U' shape, otherwise it is unlucky!

• Horse whisperers are special people who can communicate with horses and can help them overcome fear or other problems. Not much talking happens – horse and whisperer communicate using body language.